Unlocking The Mysteries Of Telepathy

The Extraordinary Power of Invisible Communication

BY MRINALINI EROOLEN

Contents

About The Author

Meet MRINALINI EROOLEN, the Invisible Master who bestows Enlightenment upon others instantly. She is an accomplished Author, Energy Healer, and Blogger.

After a decade of intense meditation, she has transcended the peak of human Consciousness, making her the only person in the world to do so.

As of 2022, she has authored over 500 books on various topics such as mindfulness, awareness, healing, and practical ways to live in the moment and life After Enlightenment.

Her mission is to share her blessings, wisdom, inner powers, and blissfulness with sincere seekers who desire a life filled with joy, serenity, and true freedom.

What Is Telepathy?

Telepathy is the ability to communicate thoughts, ideas, and flow from the invisible source between individuals without using conventional forms of communication such as speech or writing.

Indeed, telepathy is a form of communication that relies on energy rather than the use of one's voice.

While some may find it challenging, it is mainly because they lack knowledge about the telepathic process.

Telepathy is a concept that has been explored and used by many people and cultures throughout history, including some indigenous tribes and spiritual traditions.

In modern times, there are some individuals who claim to have telepathic abilities.

Some people also practice telepathy as a form of meditation or spiritual practice, while others may use it as a tool for personal growth and development.

Overall, telepathy remains a controversial and mysterious topic with varying beliefs and practices surrounding it.

The Secrets About Telepathy

There are many secrets within us that have not been discovered yet or even fully developed yet. One of them is telepathy.

Telepathy is a form of power that utilizes electric currents to establish a connection.

Telepathy can facilitate communication not only between two individuals but also among a group of people.

It also creates communication with the Ultimate Source and this is where Wisdom Flow emerges.

So, telepathy is a power in the same way as focus, observation, intuition, determination, realization, visualization are.

It's just that it is that some people use it so rarely that they think it is a miracle or it is nearly impossible to happen.

If you closely observe, you may realize that the inner powers you utilize to carry out your daily activities are often unknown to you, despite residing within you.

In the same way, there are many powers within human beings that have not been explored and developed yet.

The Advantages Of Telepathy

Telepathy is the ability to communicate through thoughts, emotions, and via the flow from the invisible source and it can offer several advantages, including the following:

Improved Communication

Telepathy can allow individuals to communicate without the limitations of language and other communication barriers.

This can improve communication between people of different cultures and languages and can be particularly useful in emergency situations when verbal communication is not possible.

Enhanced Relationships

Telepathy can enhance relationships between people, allowing them to understand each other's thoughts and emotions more deeply.

This can lead to stronger connections, greater empathy, and better problem-solving abilities.

Increased Privacy

Telepathy can provide a more private mode of communication, particularly useful in situations where verbal communication may not be appropriate or safe.

Increased Sensitivity

Telepathy can help develop a greater sensitivity to subtle energies and vibrations, leading to increased intuition and psychic abilities.

Potential for Spiritual Growth

Telepathy can also be a tool for spiritual growth, allowing individuals to access higher levels of consciousness and connect with spiritual realms.

Please note here that if you are not prepared to use telepathy, then, it is not recommended to attempt to do so.

Telepathy requires a certain level of mental and spiritual readiness, and attempting it without proper preparation can lead to confusion, frustration, or even doubts.

It is important to have a solid foundation of self-awareness, mental clarity, and spiritual grounding before attempting to use telepathy.

If you are interested in developing this ability, then, practice the technique given in this book regularly with patience and discipline.

However, you can learn how to utilize telepathy, and this guide will teach you how.

What Is The Process Of Telepathy?

Telepathy is an immensely potent means of communicating with individuals who are open to this form of communication.

Interestingly, it can be especially beneficial for those who cannot utilize conventional communication tools such as phones or the internet, particularly in challenging circumstances.

Telepathy is often subject to misunderstanding.

One common misconception is that it occurs when two individuals happen to think of each other simultaneously. However, this is an inaccurate portrayal of telepathy.

This phenomenon is actually another form of connection, one that relies on memory and cognitive processing.

When you recall someone, you activate your thought processes, enabling you to remember and connect with them on a mental level.

The strength of this cognitive recall is often so potent that it can elicit a reciprocal response from the person being remembered as if the thought has been transmitted to their mind.

Some individuals even believe that telepathy involves an emotional connection, where one person's emotional state can be communicated to another through thoughts, allowing them to understand what the person is feeling.

Yet another common misconception is that telepathy involves making assumptions or guesses about something and that being able to do so with a reasonable degree of accuracy constitutes telepathic ability.

These and other misunderstandings have resulted in a range of inaccurate beliefs and myths about telepathy.

All of these misconceptions center around the interplay of thoughts and emotions, and most people tend to focus on this aspect.

However, it is important to note that simply experiencing common occurrences does not necessarily indicate the use of telepathic ability.

Unfortunately, many individuals follow these trends and continue to propagate such misunderstandings.

Such individuals tend to conform to popular trends, leading them to believe that they can predict someone's behavior with relative accuracy.

For example, if someone is known to have a passion for drawing trees, these individuals may assume that any artwork they produce will inevitably feature trees.

In addition, even financial advisors may rely on trends to analyze and forecast future economic conditions, enabling investors to make informed decisions regarding their investments.

The reality is that true understanding comes from being fully present and conscious of the current trend, allowing for a more informed perspective on the situation at hand.

Through awareness, one can find solutions to any problem and accurately anticipate both the present and future.

Making instantaneous, well-informed decisions can only occur when one is completely conscious and aware.

This is where many financial advisors falter, as they are unable to predict the future.

Consider the current pandemic, for instance.

If one has heightened awareness regarding the origins and projected duration of the virus, what might a financial advisor have recommended to their clients before the outbreak occurred?

Where should investments be made?

Should all eggs be placed in one basket?

What trends would the advisor analyze?

Did you know that trends are often based on expectations and assumptions, rather than reality?

Life is constantly changing, and as a result, trends are not always accurate predictors of the future.

For instance, who could have anticipated that the majority of the world would be forced into confinement due to a global pandemic?

The truth is, only those who were directly involved in creating the virus truly understand it and its potential impact.

They wanted to bring about change, and as a result, it's not possible to rely solely on trends to predict what will happen next.

Any creation has the potential to bring about change, so it's difficult for anyone to predict the future with complete accuracy.

It's important to always take a step back and look at the bigger picture.

***What matters is not what you see,
but rather the perspective from
which you view it.***

This is how being true to yourself makes you not just a master of the mind, but a master in all areas.

In this state, there is no need to learn in order to speak the truth, because you are the truth itself. *How can the source learn from itself?*

The misconceptions surrounding the power of telepathy must be dispelled.

True telepathy is not based on thoughts; it exists on a higher plane.

In the following, I will explain how this genuine telepathic process operates.

How Does the Process of Real Telepathy Work?

The process of real telepathy requires certain key ingredients.

Cosmic Energy is one such energy that is essential for telepathy. Thus, thoughts, emotions, assumptions, or anything related to the mind are not needed in the process. In fact, the mind is not required at all.

Telepathy involves direct and immediate communication through a direct connection in the present moment. *So, what is required for this type of communication?*

Awareness

To communicate via telepathy, you need to enhance your level of awareness to the point where you can remain in a state of stillness and remain sharp for an extended period of time.

Motivation

Telepathy cannot be used effectively without a high level of motivation.

Right Focusing

To use telepathy effectively, you must prepare yourself with the right focus.

Simply attempting it without proper preparation will result in the use of your mind's thoughts and emotions.

Therefore, it is essential to focus on only one thing at a time with sharp focus, which can be achieved through proper preparation.

Concentration

Before attempting telepathy, it's crucial to develop the skill of concentration.

However, many people struggle to concentrate effectively. Therefore, it's essential to work on improving your concentration level before attempting telepathy.

Additionally, during telepathic communication, you need to maintain a sharp focus and gradually increase it as your telepathy journey progresses.

Visualization

Many people confuse visualization with imagination, which leads to misunderstandings.

However, visualization is directly connected to the flow of Cosmic Energy, whereas imagination is linked to the mind, thoughts, emotions, assumptions, and memories.

Visualization is a powerful tool that can produce remarkable results if utilized correctly.

Determination

If you lack sufficient determination, your telepathy journey is unlikely to be successful. As you progress on this journey, it's crucial to steadily increase your level of determination until you achieve success.

Therefore, as evident, achieving real success in telepathy requires thorough preparation.

It should be noted that telepathy is not for everyone as not everyone is willing to undergo such extensive preparation. Hence, only a handful of people can truly master it.

The Process Of Real Telepathy

Prepare yourself as I am about to explain how you can proceed with genuine telepathy.

It's important to note that for the real telepathy process to work, two individuals are required and both should be fully prepared beforehand. Without proper preparation, success in the process cannot be guaranteed.

Initially, both individuals need to communicate through telepathy simultaneously.

Once both have mastered this skill, telepathy can be performed at any time.

This implies that you can send a message through telepathy even if the other person is not in sync with you at that moment.

In this process, even if the other person is not actively connected, they will still receive the message like an alarm.

It is the same as receiving notification on their mobile device. Once they receive the message, they will reply to you and vice versa.

So, let's start.

Take a seat

Get into a comfortable sitting position and close your eyes.

Concentrate

Concentrate on the third eye. The third eye is mysterious and supernatural that refers to an invisible eye located in the center of the forehead. It is associated with intuitive perception and higher consciousness.

Intensify Energy

Intensify the energy of the third eye.

Use Visualization

When you feel the intensity of energy piercing your third eye and it feels like it's about to explode, use your visualization to see the third eye of the person you want to communicate with.

The other person must also follow the same steps.

Increase Intensity of Energy

Increase the intensity of the energy behind your third eye to allow the energy to flow out from it.

Observe

Once you feel and observe the energy coming out, visualize creating a bridge with it that connects your third eye to the other person's third eye.

Using the visualization technique, you can perceive the bridge as a thin and straight line of energy.

Improve Connection

You must focus on intensifying the energy flow in the thin line and make it thicker to improve connection and communication.

The thicker the line, the stronger the connection and the better the communication will be.

At this point, you have successfully established a connection with the other person.

After establishing the connection, you can begin your conversation. *How can you start it?*

Communication

Your communication will not be verbal, but rather through energy. There will be no sound involved as telepathy is practiced in deep silence.

Focus

Thus, you need to focus your attention on your third eye and use your consciousness and awareness to communicate.

Awareness

If one is completely aware, then their actions happen spontaneously, including speech.

Therefore, if speech can be spontaneous through awareness, why not communicate directly through awareness without speech?

<u>Realization</u>

With consistent practice, you may come to realize that communicating through awareness without speech is a viable option.

Although it may appear to be impossible at first, it can become the most effective way to communicate with others over time.

Consider the current difficult phase of life with the pandemic. *What if there were no internet, connection or electricity, how would you communicate with loved ones who are far away?*

Telepathy is a powerful tool that can connect you with loved ones, no matter where they are in the world.

Just like aura cleansing and distance healing, it does not require physical proximity or internet connection to work.

Even during difficult times like the ongoing pandemic, telepathy can be the most effective means of communication between people.

Regular Practice

With regular practice, telepathy can become a natural way of communicating through the power of awareness.

You just use your awareness directly to communicate. *How to do that?*

The Message

During this form of communication, you must focus on intensifying the energy of your third eye, create the message you wish to convey, and push it out from your third eye.

To create the message, you need to be in a state of awareness, and the message will emerge through the energy.

It's similar to how wisdom flows; you don't know what you're about to learn, but it appears through the energy.

Similarly, the message that you are going to send will be a flow of wisdom. It will be instant, only through your awareness, and extremely powerful.

Ensure that your message is traveling straight through the bridge that you have created. You can visualize it moving along the bridge and entering the third eye of the other person.

Once your message has entered the other person's third eye, they will be able to feel it.

Once the recipient recognizes your message, they will use the same process to reply to you.

Transcending Time

While it may seem difficult, with the necessary preparation mentioned earlier, it can be accomplished with regular practice.

Hence, initially, it is important for both of you to agree upon a specific time for communication.

As you both continue to practice and refine your telepathic abilities, you will eventually be able to communicate without the need for scheduling a specific time.

With telepathy, you can transcend time and communicate with one another as needed.

If you have all the necessary ingredients, you are ready to explore a new world full of inner mysteries.

Begin practicing this genuine telepathy process and you will discover how it enhances your inner powers.

Here, I have developed a unique telepathy technique with immense power that can transport you to another dimension, making you feel like you are no longer on planet Earth but in a home of your creation.

Practice this technique regularly until you have mastered it.

In my next message, I will share another powerful inner mystery with you. Until then, stay connected and receive my blessings.

Conclusion

In conclusion, telepathy is a powerful tool that can be used to communicate with others without the need for physical proximity or traditional methods of communication.

By focusing on your third eye and creating a bridge of energy between yourself and the person you want to communicate with, you can send and receive messages through awareness and energy.

While telepathy may seem difficult at first, with regular practice, it can become a natural and effortless means of communication.

Just remember to stay focused, use your intuition, and be open to the messages that come through.

With time and dedication, you can unlock the full potential of your inner powers and connect with others on a deeper, more meaningful level.